Grape Clusters (page 38)
Fruity Lemonade (page 66)
Chinese Chicken Puff (page 154)

About the Author

Penny Warner is a busy mother of two and has devoted her career to the study and teaching of child development and nutrition. She holds a master's degree in Early Childhood Education from San Francisco State University, and currently teaches child development at Diablo Valley College in the East Bay area of San Francisco.

Penny has appeared regularly on "People Are Talking", a San Francisco television show, where she has discussed and demonstrated tips for raising and living with young children. She also appears on the popular TV show, "A.M. San Francisco." She has received thousands of requests for her healthy snack ideas as a result of these appearances. Healthy Snacks for Kids has been developed in answer to these many requests.

Offer nutritious snacks, drinks and meals children will love.

- Authored by child development expert and television talk show authority Penny Warner.

- More than 200 quick and easy recipes for snacks, mini-meals, desserts, drinks, lunch-box fillers, freezer treats, and more.

- Emphasis on fresh, easy-to-find ingredients with a minimum of sugar and salt.

- Special tips for "smuggling" nutritious foods into every meal.

- For easy use this book lies flat when opened and is printed in large easy-to-read type.

- Compact design—takes a minimum of counter space.

To Tom, my loving culinary critic.
To Matthew and Rebecca, my little taste-testers.

healthy Snacks for kids

by Penny Warner

©Copyright 1983
Nitty Gritty Productions
P.O. Box 5457
Concord, California 94524-0457

A Nitty Gritty Cookbook
Printed by Mariposa Press
Concord, California

ISBN 0-911954-80-5
Library of Congress Catalog Card Number 83-061788

First Edition

Editor: Jackie Walsh
Art Director: Mike Nelson
Illustrator: Dorothy Davis
Photographer: Glen Millward
Food Stylist: Bobbie Greenlaw

Table of Contents

Introduction

"Snack time!" The words are magic to a child's ear. But to a parent, they can present a real challenge. You may reach a point where you don't know what to do to get your child to eat nutritious foods. Try as you might to introduce "high fiber" and leafy greens, your child refuses to have any part of them. You're beginning to think it's hopeless. Maybe those pre-packaged cookies and chips aren't so bad. After all, a child has to eat something!

O.K. It's definitely time for a new approach. When all else has failed, try trickery! Be sneaky with the picky eater and pump up his or her breakfasts, lunches, dinners and snacks with more nutritious ingredients. Armed with new recipes, confidence and courage, you'll soon be an expert at adding nutrients in ways "you know who" will never suspect. Many wonderful foods can be camouflaged in after-school snacks and mealtime favorites. Without even realizing it, your child will have expanded his or her taste-bud limitations, and you are gradually influencing and encouraging healthy eating. With the help of the many ideas and recipes in this collection, you can be sure you will be establishing a lifetime of good eating habits for your child.

To make your job easier, the recipes in this book are high in nutrition, easy to prepare, inexpensive, low or absent in sugar and salt, and kids love them!

◀ **Pinwheels (page 140)**

The Basics of Healthy Eating

THE 8 SECRETS TO MAKING YOUR CHILD A HEALTHY EATER

1. Smuggle nutritious foods into old favorites.

   Mix mashed peas or pureed spinach into your hamburger mix, grated carrots into peanut butter and cooked zucchini into pancakes. Add a little wheat germ to your pizza dough, biscuits and cookies. Be creative with your trickery, you'll surprise yourself.

2. Give food silly names.

   Children love whimsical things and will usually try something new if it has a funny name. What kid could resist a glass of "Mooseberry Juice" at lunch or a "U.F.O." for breakfast?

3. Let kids help.

   Even small children can help in the preparation of some of the things they eat. If a child has helped make a snack, he or she is more likely to eat it.

4. Go easy on sugar and salt.

Try to omit sugar and salt from recipes you make, or at least decrease the amount used. The results may not taste as good to you, but if your child is raised without sugar and salt, she or he will never miss them. Use alternatives, such as dates and raisins, for adding sweet flavor whenever possible. If you have to sweeten anything, use honey instead of sugar . . . only because it is sweeter and you don't need as much. Keep salt and sugar off the table, and look for unsweetened products at the market.

5. Educate your child about basic nutrition.

Talk about foods that help children grow strong and stay healthy . . . and those that don't. Classify foods at the market or on the table, into the four food groups. Play simple games that teach about these foods.

6. Serve small helpings and cut everything into small bites to fit small mouths.

It's not so overwhelming when there are small amounts on a plate. A child will ask for more if desired. Make everything look as appetizing as possible. Sometimes it's fun to make a face or a design with the bites of food. Try

Continued

anything to create a happy atmosphere and stimulate a child's imagination and desire to try the food. Ask your child to **try** everything. Don't force her or him to **finish** everything.

7. Let "props" help sell what you're serving.

Everyone knows that kids love bright colors, animals, clowns, funny straws and above all, variety. Use this knowledge when serving your child's meals. A different plate or a funny bowl with a picture on it just might stimulate a child's desire to try something new. Avoid the same old thing. Collect a variety of small colorful plates, cups, bowls, glasses and placemats.

8. Make mealtime and snack time a social event in a pleasant atmosphere.

A child is much more apt to try new things under these circumstances. Don't get angry . . . it only makes a child more stubborn about trying new foods. Maybe he or she simply isn't hungry, but will be a willing-eater at the next meal. Try to avoid pleading ("Please eat"), threatening ("No dessert if you don't eat your salad") or guilt-inducing ("Think of all the hungry children in the world"), they won't help.

THE "HEALTHY" FOODS

This is a list of good basic foods children should be encouraged to eat. If a child learns to enjoy them early he or she will be a healthy eater for life.

Use these foods interchangeably in the recipes in this book, and the recipes as a guideline for your own ideas. Instead of sneaking spinach into hamburgers (Popeye Burgers, page 178) hide pureed peas or green beans in meat loaf mix.

Good Basic Foods (for everyday)

milk	brussels sprouts	peaches
eggs	carrots	peas
cheese	citrus fruits	potatoes
liver	green leafy vegetables	squash
apricots	green peppers	sweet potatoes
broccoli	melons	tomatoes

Foods To Cut Down On or Avoid

fats   salt   sugar

Continued

Foods High in Fiber (your child should have lots of them)

apples	coconut	potato skins
apricots	corn	prunes
bananas	dates	raisins
beans	green beans	raspberries
bran cereals	nuts	spinach
broccoli	pears	strawberries
carrots	peas	whole grain breads
cherries	plums	

Substitution Suggestions

Carob powder is a good substitute for chocolate.

Whole wheat flour can be substituted for white flour in most recipes. If you don't want to use all whole wheat, replace part of the white flour with whole wheat flour. You will be adding important fiber to your family's diet.

Use whole grain bread whenever possible.

Fruit Bricks (page 19) ▶
Peanut Butter Dates (page 29)

Snacks: Quick, Easy and Delicious!

SUPER SNACKS

Snacks are an important and necessary part of a child's life. Because of the enormous amounts of energy used, little bodies need refueling between meals. This important role that snacks play in keeping children healthy makes it all the more necessary that they be as nutritious as possible, and something your child will love to eat.

Keeping in mind that foods which are good for children are not necessarily the ones they will eat, the snacks carefully chosen for this chapter pack a lot of extra nutrition into good foods kids do like, and disguise less popular ones by hiding them in old favorites.

These delicious snacks are great anytime—mid-morning, after school, before a late dinner, and at bedtime. They are also great additions to breakfast, lunch and dinner.

With the wide variety of recipes in this chapter, you'll have enough new snacks to last a long time!

Banana Chips

This is so easy!

4 bananas

1/4 cup lemon juice

Slice bananas and dip into lemon juice. Place on greased cookie sheet in a single layer. Bake at 175ºF. for 2-3 hours, or until golden. Makes 2 to 4 servings.

Cheese Stacks

Refrigerate any leftovers.

1/4 cup margarine
1/2 cup grated cheese

2 cups spoon-size snredded wheat

Melt margarine and cheese in a large saucepan over medium heat. When just melted, add shredded wheat. Stir to coat thoroughly. Spread out on foil to cool.

Fruit Bricks

Children can play with this snack and eat it too!

3 envelopes unflavored gelatin
3/4 cup boiling water

1 can (12 ozs.) frozen apple, orange **or** grape juice concentrate

Dissolve gelatin in boiling water. Add juice and stir until mixed. Pour into lightly buttered 9- x 13-inch pan. Chill for several hours. Cut into squares for building blocks or use cookie cutters to make interesting shapes to play with.

Munchkins

1 cup dried apricots, chopped
1 cup pecans, chopped

2 tbs. orange juice

Steam apricots in a strainer or steamer basket over boiling water for 5 minutes or until softened. Combine apricots, pecans and orange juice in a small bowl. Stir until well mixed. Shape into balls and refrigerate.

Sidewalk Mix

There aren't a lot of trails in the suburbs, so we call it "sidewalk mix"!

2 cups granola
1/2 cup coconut
1/2 cup chopped dates

1/4 cup chopped peanuts
2 tbs. honey (if desired)

Mix all ingredients and press into pan. Cut into small pieces. Or, omit honey and serve in a large bowl. Makes 4 servings.

Hot Nibbles

1 tbs. margarine, melted
1/4 cup walnuts
1/4 cup raisins
1/4 cup sunflower seeds

1/4 cup coconut
1/4 cup dates
1/4 cup rolled oats

Stir ingredients together in skillet until heated. Serve warm.

Grandma's Wholesome Candy

Is there really such a thing as wholesome candy? Yes, but leave off the word "wholesome" when you serve it to the kids.

1/2 cup peanut butter
1/4 cup honey
1/2 cup instant nonfat dry milk (or more as needed to hold shape)

Mix peanut butter and honey. Add instant milk until you have a dough-like consistency (not too dry but not sticky). Roll into balls and place on waxed paper, or press into a pan lined with waxed paper. Cut into squares, or roll into log shape and cut into thin slices. Keep in refrigerator or freeze. Makes 24.

For variety add:

raisins	coconut	corn flakes
nuts	carob chips	Rice Krispies
sunflower seeds	wheat germ	granola
	cinnamon	

Nutty Fruit Balls

For a change, you may want to chop extra nuts or fruits to roll these balls in. A food processor makes quick work of the chopping.

1/4 cup cashews
1/4 cup walnuts
1/4 cup almonds
1/4 cup sunflower seeds
1/4 cup raisins
1/4 cup dried apricots
1/4 cup coconut
1/4 cup rolled oats
2 tbs. honey (if desired)
1/4 cup peanut butter

Chop all the nuts, seeds and fruit. Add honey and peanut butter and mix well. Roll into balls and chill.

Rabbit Sherbet (page 98) ▶
Mouse Traps (page 25)

Seed Slices

Plant a few seeds and watch your child grow!

1/2 cup carob chips
1/4 cup honey (or less if desired)
1/2 cup peanut butter
1/4 cup wheat germ
1/4 cup walnuts
1/2 cup sunflower seeds
1/2 cup sesame seeds **or** coconut

Mix all ingredients except sesame seeds or coconut. Form mixture into a roll. Chill in refrigerator for about an hour. Slice roll into 1/4-inch thick slices. Press slices into seeds or coconut. Keep refrigerated when not eating!

Mouse Traps

Leave these out if you want to catch some "little mice." Best served warm.

1 cup flour
1 cup shredded Cheddar cheese
1/2 cup soft butter or margarine

dash salt (if desired)
1/2 tsp. Worcestershire sauce (if desired)

Combine all ingredients in bowl and knead to form dough. Chill for half an hour. Shape into balls allowing 1 teaspoon per ball. Place on ungreased cookie sheet 2-inches apart. Flatten with a fork. Bake at 350°F. 12 minutes.

Cheese Leather

1 cup firm cheese, shredded or cut into chunks (Cheddar is best)

Spread cheese onto a non-stick pan. Heat in 300°F. oven until cheese melts into a thin sheet. Remove from pan with a fork and tear into strips to serve.

Jerky Popcorn

Got a meat-hating popcorn-lover? Try this sneak attack.

1 package beef jerky, chopped   2 quarts popped popcorn
1 tbs. butter

Saute jerky in butter in small frying pan. Pour over popcorn. Toss to mix well.

Peanut Butter Popcorn

Lots of fiber and peanut butter makes it more nutritious.

1 tbs. peanut butter   2 quarters popped popcorn
1 tbs. butter

Melt peanut butter and butter in small pan over low heat. Pour over popcorn. Toss to mix well. Serve with plenty of napkins.

Nutty Popcorn

Take an old favorite and load it up with protein.

1 cup chopped nuts (almonds, walnuts,
   pecans or peanuts)
1 cup sunflower seed
1/4 cup honey
1/4 cup water
1/4 cup butter

1 tbs. vanilla
1/2 tsp. salt
1 tsp. wheat germ
1 quart popped popcorn
1 cup raisins

Mix nuts and seeds. Set aside. Stir honey and water together over medium heat until candy thermometer registers 250°F. Add butter, vanilla, salt and wheat germ. Pour over popcorn in a large bowl and mix well. Spread mixture into a large baking pan. Bake at 300°F. for 15 minutes. Remove from oven. Stir in raisins. Return to oven and bake 15 minutes longer. Cool and serve in small bowls or sacks, or form into small balls.

Date Cookies

If desired, use peanut butter instead of jam.

1 cup dates, chopped
1 cup graham cracker crumbs
1/4 cup plum jam (or strawberry)
1/2 cup chopped walnuts
1/2 cup flaked coconut

Combine dates, crumbs, jam and nuts. Drop by teaspoonfuls into bowl of coconut and roll into balls. Cover and chill.

Note: If you feel that jam and jelly are too high in sugar, try one of the new "spreads." Some contain 50% less sugar, others have substituted artifical sweeteners.

Peanut Butter Dates

Try a variety of seeds and nuts if you're out of Rice Krispies.

1 cup peanut butter
1/2 cup Rice Krispies

1 package (8 ozs.) pitted dates

Mix peanut butter with Rice Krispies (or seeds, coconut, wheat germ, oatmeal). Stuff into dates. Store in refrigerator.

Peanut Butter Pudding

A high-protein, low-sugar dessert.

1 banana, cut into chunks
1/2 cup plain yogurt

1/2 cup peanut butter

Combine all ingredients in blender container. Blend until smooth. Pour into serving dishes and refrigerate. Makes 2 servings.

Bugs On A Log

Here are several ways to serve up the "bugs"...

Logs: celery stalks
      apples, halved and hollowed or quartered
      carrot sticks

Spread: pineapple cheese spread
        American cheese spread
        peanut butter
        deviled ham spread
        deviled egg spread

Bugs: raisins
      golden raisins
      carob chips
      peanuts

Prepare logs. Top with spread. Sprinkle with "bugs."

**Peanut Butter Popcorn, Jerky Popcorn (page 26)
Nutty Popcorn (page 27)** ▶

Spumoni Celery

A tricky way to cover the vegetable group. Try other combinations for variety.

1 raw carrot, finely chopped
1/4 cup finely chopped green pepper
1/2 cup cottage cheese

1/4 cup Parmesan cheese
6 celery stalks, cut into
   3- to 4-inch pieces

Mix carrot, green pepper, cottage cheese and Parmesan together well. Stuff celery pieces.

Spumoni Celery No. 2

1 banana, mashed
3 tbs. peanut butter
1 tsp. sunflower seeds

1 tsp. honey (if desired)
1 tbs. chopped almonds

Combine ingredients and stuff celery pieces.

Jack's Bean Stalks

Cheese and beans make a high-protein snack for after .

1 can (16 ozs.) kidney beans
1/2 cup grated Cheddar cheese
1/2 tsp. chili powder (if desired)
8 celery stalks

Drain the beans and save a little liquid. Mash beans with a fork, process in food processor or blend in blender, adding a little bean liquid for a creamier texture. Stir in cheese and chili powder. Simmer over low heat until cheese melts. Refrigerate. When cooled, stuff celery stalks with mixture. Cut into bite-size pieces. Keep refrigerated in airtight containers, ready for ''after-school snackers.''

Variation: Use American cheese spread instead of Cheddar cheese. Just blend the spread with the beans, season and fill celery stalks. No heating necessary.

Banana Wiggles

Gelatin is such a good package for presenting almost any food to kids.

1-1/2 packages unflavored gelatin
1 cup boiling water
1 cup strawberry puree **or** 1 can (6 ozs.) strawberry nectar
3/4 cup cold water
bananas
popsicle sticks
orange juice cans **or** large plastic cups
aluminum foil

Dissolve gelatin in boiling water. Add strawberry puree or nectar and cold water. Chill in refrigerator until slightly thickened. Peel bananas and cut in half. Insert a popsicle stick in one end of each banana. Place bananas in orange juice cans or large plastic cups, stick-ends up. Pour in gelatin. To keep stick centered, place foil over top of can with slit in the middle for stick. Chill in refrigerator several hours. To loosen, dip cans in warm water for a few seconds. Wiggle gently to remove.

Fruit Leather

Surprisingly easy and a lot of fun to make but be sure to pick a sunny day. Let the kids help. Use your food processor or blender to puree the fruit.

2-1/2 cups fruit puree (no pits, but leave the peels—try plums, apricots, peaches, apples, nectarines, strawberries)
2 tbs. honey (if desired)
1/2 tsp. lemon juice

Combine all ingredients in medium-size saucepan. Bring to a boil over medium-high heat. Stir as you cook. When the mixture thickens, remove from heat and let it cool slightly. In the meantime, cover a jelly roll pan (or cookie sheet with sides) with Saran Wrap (or other **heavy duty** plastic wrap) and tape it to the pan. Pour mixture over wrap and let it spread by itself to approximately 1/4-inch thick. Place in bright sunlight for two to three days, until it is no longer tacky. (Cover at night or bring inside.) When dry, roll up in wrap and store in refrigerator. It will keep for months, I've been told. With children around it disappears in a hurry.

Strawberry Pudding

You can make your own delicious pudding with only a little honey! Try other fresh fruit for variety.

1 can (6 ozs.) frozen apple juice concentrate, thawed
2 cans water
1 tbs. honey (if desired)
1/4 cup cornstarch
2 cups fresh strawberries, chopped

Combine juice, water, honey and cornstarch. Cook over medium heat, stirring constantly, until mixture thickens and boils. Add strawberries and boil one minute, stirring constantly. Remove from heat and pour into individual dishes. Makes 4 servings.

Apple Boats

Three food groups are covered with these delicious, high-protein snacks.

6 green apples
1 cup peanut butter, chunky-style preferred
1/2 cup peanuts, chopped
1/2 cup Rice Krispies
1/4 cup raisins
Cheddar cheese

Cut apples in half and remove cores, leaving hollows for the peanut butter mixture. Mix peanut butter with peanuts, Rice Krispies and raisins. Spoon into prepared apples. Cut into slices for small children. Make sails with triangles of cheese.

Variation: Substitute shredded or chopped carrots for raisins.

Grape Clusters

Not that grapes need dressing up, but this is quite an eye-catcher.

1 bunch of grapes
4 sqs. (4 ozs.) semi-sweet chocolate

1/2 cup finely chopped walnuts

Cut grapes into clusters of about 3 to 5 grapes. Melt chocolate. Dip grapes into melted chocolate, then into chopped walnuts. Chill in refrigerator.

Banana Oatsies

A good fruit 'n' cereal snack.

4 bananas
1/2 cup oats

1-1/2 cups chopped walnuts
1 tsp. vanilla

Mash bananas and add other ingredients. Mix well. Drop by teaspoonfuls onto ungreased cookie sheet. Bake at 350°F. 20 to 25 minutes. Makes 2-1/2 dozen.

Fruit Cobbler Crunch (page 40)
Seed Slices (page 24) ▶

Fruit Cobbler Crunch

This is a quick and easy way to serve fruit. Use fruits canned in their own juice without added sugar, if possible.

1 can (8 ozs.) peaches, pears, apricots **or** plums
1 tsp. cinnamon

2 tbs. granola
2 tbs. plain **or** fruit yogurt

Drain fruit. Rinse lightly if packed in heavy syrup. Slice into serving dishes. Sprinkle cinnamon on top. Add granola and top with yogurt. Makes 2 servings.

Pita Parfait

How about a "fruit sandwich"?

1 can (8 ozs.) fruit cocktail, drained
2 tbs. cottage cheese

1 tbs. chopped almonds **or** walnuts
1 pita bread

Mix fruit with cottage cheese and nuts. Spoon into pita pocket.

Oven Apples

Baked apples, child-size. Perfect for breakfast, lunch, dinner or a snack.

4 small baking apples
2 tbs. chopped walnuts

2 tbs. raisins
1 tsp. cinnamon

Cut apples in half and hollow out core. Place in baking pan. Combine nuts, raisins and cinnamon in a small bowl. Stuff into apple hollows. Cover and bake at 350°F. 30 minutes. Serve at room temperature or chilled. Makes 4 to 8 servings.

Super-Hero Snacks

2 eggs   1/2 cup unsweetened applesauce   2 cups granola

Beat eggs well and blend into applesauce. Add granola and stir well until mixed. Spread in 8-inch square pan that is lightly buttered. Press firmly into pan. Bake at 350°F. for 20 minutes. Cut into bars and serve.

Apple Smacks

Served warm or cold, it's always a favorite.

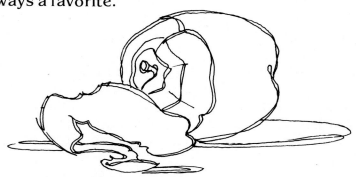

4 apples, sliced
1/4 cup raisins
1/4 cup water
3/4 cup rolled oats
1/3 cup flour
1/4 cup wheat germ (if desired)
1/4 cup margarine
2 tbs. honey (if desired)
1 tsp. cinnamon

Lay apple slices in greased 8-inch square pan. Combine remaining ingredients and sprinkle over apples. Bake at 350°F. for 35 minues. Spoon into small dishes and top with yogurt, if desired. Makes 4 servings.

Yogurt Plus

Here's an easy way to cover the four food groups—(1) Fruits and Vegetables, (2) Protein, (3) Cereals and (4) Dairy —in one delicious snack! The following are just a few suggestions; there are many more which you will want to add.

To yogurt add one of the following from each food group. Mix and match.

Strawberries	(1)	Shredded carrots	(1)
Raspberries	(1)	Chopped raw vegetables	(1)
Blueberries	(1)	Sunflower seeds	(2)
Apricots	(1)	Walnuts	(2)
Chopped apples	(1)	Rice Krispies	(3)
Sliced bananas	(1)	Grapenuts	(3)
Orange sections	(1)	Granola	(3)
Raisins	(1)	Brown rice	(3)
Melon cubes	(1)	Whole wheat croutons	(3)

Sprinkle the fruit mixtures with cinnamon, if desired.

Cheese Straws

This snack is easy and makes a lot. Store extras in the freezer. Pie crust mix is used to save time, but if you have a favorite pie crust recipe, use it.

1/2 cup shredded Cheddar cheese
2 tbs. wheat germ
1 package pie crust mix

Make pie crust according to package directions. Roll the crust out on a floured board into a rectangle about 1/4-inch thick. Sprinkle half the rectangle with the cheese and wheat germ. Fold the other half over cheese and roll to 1/4-inch thick. Cut the dough into strips, 1/2 by 3 inches. Place on greased cookie sheet and bake at 400°F. for 12 to 15 minutes. Watch carefully and don't over-brown. Makes 2 dozen.

Cheese Sticks

Keep these handy for satisfying between-meal snacks.

1 cup flour
1 tsp. cinnamon
1 tsp. baking soda
1/4 cup butter
3/4 cup grated Cheddar cheese
1 egg, beaten
1 tbs. milk

Mix flour, cinnamon and soda. Cut in butter and cheese until mixture becomes crumbly. Beat egg and milk together. Add to flour mixture and stir until dough-like consistency. With lighty floured hands, roll teaspoonfuls of dough into sticks. Place 1-inch apart on ungreased cookie sheet. Bake at 375°F. for 8 to 10 minutes. Makes 1 dozen.

Hot Cheese Funnies

This is a New York City special! For a super treat, dip warm pretzels in melted cheese or a soft cheese spread.

1 package dry yeast
1-1/2 cups warm water (105° to 115°F.)
3-1/2 cups flour
1 cup grated Cheddar cheese
1 egg

Dissolve yeast in water. Stir in flour and cheese. Knead dough until smooth. (Add more flour a teaspoon at a time, if too sticky.) Break off walnut-sized pieces and roll into 12-inch long ropes. Twist into pretzel shapes or let the kids make a few shapes of their own. Place on ungreased cookie sheet and brush with beaten egg. Bake at 425°F. 15 to 20 minutes. Serve warm.

"Add Too" Suggestions (page 139) ▶

Cocobars

Chewy and delicious. Great for a Scout or Brownie meeting.

1 can (20 ozs.) crushed pineapple
1 egg
2 cups coconut
3/4 cup flour
1/4 cup wheat germ

Drain pineapple, reserving 3/4 cup juice. Beat egg in mixing bowl. Add pineapple juice and beat until blended. Add pineapple and coconut. Stir in flour and wheat germ. Pour batter into greased 8-inch square pan. Bake at 350°F. for 40 minutes. Cool and cut into bars about 1-1/4 by 2 inches. Makes 24 bars.

Fruit Chewies

These snacks are high in fiber and naturally sweet.

3 ripe bananas
1 cup chopped dates
1/4 cup oil
2 cups oats

1/2 cup chopped walnuts,
 peanuts, **or** pecans
1 tsp. vanilla

Cut two bananas into medium-size chunks. Mash the third banana. Combine all ingredients and stir until mixed. Let stand for 10 minutes. Drop by teaspoonfuls onto greased cookie sheet. Bake at 350ºF. for 15 to 20 minutes. Makes 2 dozen.

Hawaiian Rollers

A quick and easy energy-giving snack for a hungry soccer team. Maybe you should double the recipe!

1 can (8 ozs.) refrigerated crescent rolls
1/2 cup pineapple preserves (less if desired)
1/2 tsp. cinnamon
1/4 cup coconut
1/4 cup walnuts, chopped

Separate dough into two long rectangles. Divide preserves and spread evenly over each rectangle. Sprinkle evenly with cinnamon, coconut and nuts. Roll up dough lengthwise, and seal. Cut each roll into 1/2-inch slices. Place cut-side up on ungreased cookie sheet. Bake at 350°F. for 10 minutes. Serve warm or cooled. Makes 24.

Apricotties

1/2 cup dried apricots, chopped
1/2 cup raisins
1/2 cup dates, chopped
1 can (6 ozs.) frozen orange juice concentrate
1-1/2 cups oats
1 cup flour
1 tsp. baking soda
dash salt (if desired)
1 egg
1/2 cup vegetable oil
1/4 cup sunflower seeds

Combine apricots, raisins, dates and orange juice in a saucepan. Simmer over low heat for 10 minutes, stirring occasionally. Remove from heat and cool. Stir together oats, flour, baking soda, egg and oil. Mix until well blended. Stir in fruit mixture and seeds. Form into small balls and place 2 inches apart on a baking sheet which has been covered with foil. Flatten to 1/4-inch and bake at 350°F. for 10 minutes. Cool. Makes 1-1/2 dozen.

Banana Bombs

Great for outings and picnics

1 cup flour
1/2 tsp. baking soda
1/2 tsp. salt (if desired)
1/2 cup chopped nuts or seeds
1 banana, cut into small chunks
1 egg
1 tsp. vanilla

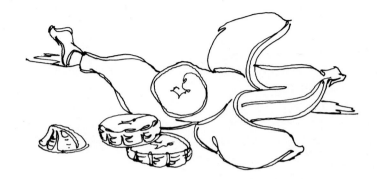

Combine flour, soda, salt and nuts in mixing bowl. Set aside. Combine banana, dates, egg and vanilla in blender. Blend until smooth. Add to dry ingredients and mix well. Drop by teaspoonfuls onto greased cookie sheet. Flatten with back of spoon. Bake at 350°F. for 10 minutes. Makes 2 dozen.

Carob Circles

When the requests are for chocolate, make these.

1 cup chopped dates
2 eggs
1 tsp. vanilla
3 tbs. carob powder
1 cup flour
1/2 tsp. baking powder
1/4 tsp. salt (if desired)
1/2 tsp. cinnamon
1/2 cup chopped walnuts

Combine dates, eggs, vanilla and carob in blender container. Blend well on high speed. Pour into mixing bowl. Add flour, baking powder, salt and cinnamon. Stir until well mixed. Add walnuts. Shape into balls and place on greased cookie sheet, 2 inches apart. Flatten with tines of fork or back of spoon. Bake at 350°F. for 8 to 10 minutes. Makes 2 dozen.

Cupcones

These go over big at birthday or classroom parties.

24 ice cream cup cones
1/2 cup peanut butter
1/3 cup margarine
2 to 4 tbs. honey
2 eggs
1 tsp. vanilla

2 cups flour
1/2 tsp. salt (if desired)
2-1/2 tsp. baking powder
3/4 cup milk
jam or yogurt
coconut, raisins or chopped nuts

Place cones in muffin tins. Combine peanut butter and margarine. Add honey and beat until fluffy. Beat in eggs and vanilla. Add flour, salt, baking powder and milk. Beat until mixed. Spoon into cones to about 1/4-inch from the top. Bake at 350°F. for 25 minutes. Frost with jam or yogurt and sprinkle with coconut (colored, if desired), raisins, or chopped nuts.

Nutter Butter Cookies

These cookies freeze well if they aren't all eaten first.

1 cup apple butter
1/2 cup peanut butter
1 tsp. vanilla
3/4 cup instant nonfat dry milk
3/4 cup flour
1/4 tsp. cinnamon
1/2 cup raisins

Beat apple butter, peanut butter and vanilla together in mixing bowl. Add milk, flour, cinnamon and raisins. Mix well. Drop by teaspoonfuls onto greased cookie sheet. Flatten with tines of a fork. Bake at 350°F. for 10 minutes. Serve warm, or chill in refrigerator. Makes 2-1/2 dozen.

Monkey Bars

A well-rounded breakfast, too!

1/2 cup margarine, softened
1/4 cup honey (or less if desired)
1 egg
1/4 tsp. cinnamon
1 banana
4 cups oats
1/2 cup chopped dried apricots
1/2 cup chopped prunes
1/2 cup raisins
1/2 cup chopped walnuts
1/2 cup sunflower seeds

Beat margarine and honey until light and fluffy. Add egg, cinnamon and bananas and beat well. Stir in remaining ingredients and spread into greased 9- by 13-inch pan. Bake at 350°F. for 50 minutes. Cool and cut into squares.

Snap and Crackle Cookies

Another tricky way to get breakfast down their throats.

1 cup flour
1/2 tsp. baking powder
1/4 tsp. salt (if desired)
3/4 cup butter, softened
1/4 cup honey (or less if desired)
1 egg
1/2 tsp. vanilla
1 cup Rice Krispies
1/2 cup chopped walnuts

Sift flour, baking powder and salt together. Cream butter and honey until light and fluffy. Beat in egg and vanilla. Add flour mixture and blend well. Stir in Rice Krispies and nuts. Drop by tablespoonfuls onto greased cookie sheet, about 2 inches apart. Bake at 375°F. for 10 minutes. Allow to cool. Makes 24.

Whole Wheat Brownies

If your kids just can't live without an occasional brownie, try these instead. You can always add one-half cup shredded carrots or zucchini, but don't tell anyone.

1/2 cup margarine, softened
1/4 cup honey
2 squares unsweetened chocolate, melted and cooled
2 eggs
1 tsp. vanilla
1/2 cup whole wheat flour
1/2 tsp. baking powder
1/4 tsp. salt (if desired)
1/2 cup chopped walnuts

Cream margarine and honey together until fluffy. Beat in chocolate, eggs and vanilla. Stir in flour, baking powder, salt and nuts. Spread in buttered 8-inch square pan. Bake in 350°F. oven for 20 minutes. Cool and cut into squares.

DYNAMITE DRINKS

It's amazing what you can sneak into a drink and get away with! As long as you blend the ingredients well in a blender and serve chilled, your child will never suspect what's making his or her drink taste so delicious. And, you can provide a complete meal in one glass. Add extra fruit, vegetables, an egg or wheat germ to anything you're preparing for your child. This idea is to pack as much good nutrition as possible into whatever your child is eating and drinking. Anytime you can add a little something extra, do it!

Serve drinks in a way that will be especially appealing to your child. Buy some new mugs with his or her favorite characters on them to use when you offer a new drink. Or serve it in one of your special champagne or wine glasses as an added treat. Scooped out orange shells are another way to dress up a drink and you don't have to wash the glass! Children love "crazy" straws that look like complex freeway overpasses. It's great fun to watch the different colored beverages flow through.

Given creative, colorful foods and an interesting atmosphere, eating can be great fun too!

V-3 Juice

It's worth a try, isn't it?

1/4 cup chopped celery
1/4 cup coarsely grated peeled carrot

1/4 cup any other vegetable
1 cup tomato juice

Combine ingredients in blender container. Blend until smooth. Serve immediately or chill before serving. Makes 1 to 2 servings.

Orange Plus Two

A pleasant change from the usual morning glass of orange juice.

1 cup orange juice
1 cup cranberry juice cocktail

1 cup club soda
ice to fill glasses

Mix orange juice, cranberry juice and soda together in a pitcher. Fill glasses with ice and pour juice over ice. Makes 2 to 4 servings.

Arctic Orange (page 91)
Tuna Boat (page 136) ▶
Apricotties (page 51)
Breakfast Shake (page 75)

Simple Simon Cider

Perfect for a cold winter evening, or a nice change for the lunchbox thermos.

3 cinnamon sticks
1 can (46 ozs.) natural apple juice
1 can (12 ozs.) apricot nectar

Combine all ingredients in large saucepan and bring to a boil. Simmer 10 minutes. Serve warm. Makes 6 servings.

Fruit Fizzie

If you are using fruit nectar, mix equal parts nectar and water.

1 can (6 ozs.) frozen juice concentrate (orange, grape or apple)
4 bottles (10 ozs. ea.) Calistoga, Perrier or other unflavored bubble water

Mix frozen concentrate with bubble water. Serve in frosty glasses.

Fruit Juicie

Makes enough for the whole neighborhood.

1 pint strawberries
2 tbs. lemon juice
3 cups boiling water

3 cups cold water
1/2 cup orange juice
crushed ice

Combine half of strawberries, lemon juice and boiling water in blender container. Blend until smooth. Pour into large bowl or pitcher. Blend remaining half and add to first mixture. Stir in cold water and orange juice. Chill. Serve over crushed ice.

Surprise Shake

The surprise—you can't taste the wheat germ and it adds so much!

6 tbs. orange juice concentrate
1 cup milk

2 tsp. wheat germ
3 ice cubes

Combine in blender container. Blend until frothy.

Fruity Lemonade

You may substitute reconstituted, frozen lemonade if you prefer. Use raspberries, blackberries, boysenberries, strawberries or a combination.

2 large lemons
1/2 cup honey (less if desired)

3-1/2 cups water
1 cup fresh **or** thawed frozen berries

Squeeze lemons into large mixing bowl. Stir in honey gradually to taste. Add water and berries. Pour into glasses and serve.

Graham Cracker Foamy

This makes a good breakfast drink, too.

1-1/2 cups milk
1 egg
2 graham crackers, broken

1/2 tsp. honey (if desired)
2 tbs. frozen orange juice concentrate

Combine ingredients in blender container. Blend until smooth and frothy.

Mighty Milk

Honestly! You can't taste the buttermilk.

1 can(6 ozs.) frozen orange
  juice concentrate

2 cups buttermilk
1 tsp. honey

Combine all ingredients in blender container. Blend. Serve over ice.

Jersey Juice

Juice and milk? Surprisingly good!

1 can (6 ozs.) frozen orange juice concentrate
2-1/2 cups milk

Combine ingredients in blender container. Blend until frothy.

Orange Jubilee

Add a little water if the blender won't turn.

1 can (6 ozs.) orange juice
concentrate, softened
1/3 cup instant nonfat dry milk

1/2 tsp. vanilla
ice cubes—enough to fill blender

Pour orange juice concentrate into blender. Add instant milk and blend until mixed. Add vanilla and ice cubes and blend on high speed until smooth.

New York "Egg Cream"

Only in New York would a drink called Egg Cream be made without eggs or cream! A legend!

1 cup club soda
1 cup milk

1 tbs. chocolate syrup **or** 1 tsp. carob
   powder **and** 1 tsp. honey

Combine in blender container. Blend on high speed until frothy. Serve with a hot pretzel! Makes 2 servings.

Eggnog Eggstacy

2 eggs
2 cups milk

1 tsp. vanilla
1/4 tsp. nutmeg

Boil the eggs for 1 minute. Pour milk and vanilla into blender container. Break eggs and add to milk. Blend on high speed until smooth and frothy. Pour into chilled glasses and sprinkle with nutmeg. Makes 2 servings.

Mooseberry Juice

Any time you can sneak in a little wheat germ, do!

1 carton (10 ozs.) frozen raspberries
1-1/2 cups milk

2 eggs
1 tbs. wheat germ

Combine ingredients in the blender container. Blend until smooth.

Flullato

This is a favorite from Italy. Use berries, peaches, apricots, pears or melon.

2/3 cup milk
2/3 cup fresh fruit, cut into pieces

1 tsp. honey (if desired)
1/4 cup crushed ice

Combine ingredients in blender container. Blend on high speed until smooth and frothy. Makes 2 servings.

Four Fruit Float

So refreshing! Use fresh or frozen berries.

1/2 cup strawberries
1/2 cup raspberries
1/2 cup blueberries

1/2 cup milk
1 cup apple juice

Measure all ingredients into blender container. Blend until smooth. Makes 4 servings.

Monkey Milkshake

This is a meal in a glass. Even those who don't like milk will ask for more.

1 cup strawberries
1 banana
1 egg

1 cup milk
2 tsp. vanilla
3 ice cubes

Combine ingredients in blender container. Blend until smooth and fluffy.

Boysenberry Blitz

This is very refreshing on a warm day. Serve in frosty glasses.

1 cup milk   1 carton (8 ozs.) boysenberry yogurt

Combine in blender container. Blend until frothy.

Variation: For a boysenberry milkshake, combine 1 cup frozen boysenberries, 1 cup vanilla ice cream and 1/4 cup milk in blender container. Blend until smooth.

Florida Frosty

1 cup orange juice   1/2 cup plain yogurt   1 banana

Combine ingredients in blender container. Blend until smooth. Serve immediately in frosty cold glasses.

◄ Hawaiian Shake (page 77)
Banana Chocolate Froth (page 76)
Boysenberry Blitz (page 73)

Blender Berries

Choose your favorite—strawberries, blueberries or boysenberries.

1/2 cup plain yogurt
2 tbs. water
1 cup fresh **or** frozen berries
1 banana

1 tbs. wheat germ
1/8 tsp. cinnamon
1/4 tsp. lemon juice

Combine ingredients in blender container. Blend until smooth. Serve chilled in frosty glasses.

Peach Fuzz

1 banana
2 ripe peaches **or** 3 canned peach halves
2 cups milk

1 carton (8 ozs.) plain yogurt
1/2 tsp. vanilla
5 ice cubes

Combine all ingredients in blender container. Blend until smooth and frothy.

Breakfast Shake

Add a strip of bacon and you have a complete breakfast!

2 cups nonfat milk
1/2 cup plain yogurt
1 egg
1 tbs. vanilla

2 tsp. nutmeg
1 cup instant nonfat dry milk
1 banana
1 can (6 ozs.) frozen orange juice concentrate

Place all ingredients in blender container. Blend until frothy.

Apple Shake

Substitute other fruit juices for variety.

1 cup vanilla ice milk
1/2 cup apple juice

1/4 tsp. cinnamon

Place all ingredients in blender container. Blend until smooth and frothy.

Banana Smoothy

Make a bet with your child that she or he can *drink* a whole banana.

1-1/2 cups lowfat milk
1 large banana

1/4 tsp. vanilla
1/2 scoop vanilla ice milk

Combine ingredients in blender container. Blend until smooth and creamy.

Banana Chocolate Froth

You can substitute two tablespoons cocoa and one teaspoon honey for the ice cream but it won't be as creamy.

1 cup milk
1 banana

1/2 to 1 cup chocolate ice cream

Combine ingredients in blender container. Blend until smooth and creamy.

Frosty Fruit Float

It doesn't take much ice milk to make this drink special.

1/4 cup fruit juice (orange, grape, cranberry, pineapple)
1 tbs. vanilla ice milk
1 bottle (10 ozs.) club soda

Pour juice into a tall glass. Add ice milk. Fill with club soda. Stir and serve.

Hawaiian Shake

Sprinkle coconut on top as a garnish.

2 cups crushed pineapple
2 cups milk

1 pint vanilla ice milk
1 tbs. lemon juice

Combine ingredients in blender container. Blend until smooth.

Grape Slush

A favorite!

1/4 cup frozen grape juice concentrate
1/4 cup frozen orange juice concentrate
1/2 cup milk
1/2 cup vanilla ice milk
1 banana

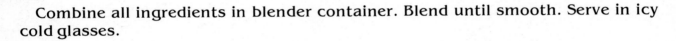

Combine all ingredients in blender container. Blend until smooth. Serve in icy cold glasses.

Note: Many of the canned fruits today are available without added sugar. Look for labels that say "lite," "diet," or "packed in its own fruit juice." Some have no sugar, others have reduced the amount by 50%.

Blender Berries (page 74) ▶

FROZEN FUN

Frozen snacks are extremely popular with kids all year long. They are a great way to disguise unpopular fruits and vegetables. Your child doesn't have to know how Rabbit Sherbet got its name. Sugar should be kept to a minimum in a child's diet, but it doesn't have to be avoided altogether. A little jam for flavor, or sherbet or ice milk, combined with other nutritious ingredients can become a special frozen treat which most children are sure to eat.

The main object of all the recipes in this book is to help you make your child's diet as healthy as possible. Since snacks are a big part of that diet, they are a great vehicle for packing healthy foods into favorites a child will eat. The snacks in this chapter are easy to make, taste great and are a whole lot more nutritious than the frozen "colored sugar water" you can buy at the supermarket. And, probably a lot less expensive, too.

Eskimo Fruit

Sometimes just making it cold makes it taste better!

Freeze fruit leather
Freeze grapes, pineapple, peaches, apricots, bananas, apples
Scoop out melon balls and freeze

King Kong's Chips

These treats only take minutes and the kids can help.

2 bananas, peeled and sliced
1/2 cup orange juice
1/2 cup wheat germ **or** coconut

Dip banana slices into orange juice, then into wheat germ or coconut. Arrange in cake pans or on plates in a single layer. Cover with plastic and freeze.

Frostbite Blizzard

ice cubes
fruit nectar, fruit juice or fruit puree

Crush ice in a heavy plastic bag with a hammer or use blender or food processor to make "snow." Scoop into bowl. Pour fruit juice or puree over "snow" and serve with spoon.

Frozen Fruit Nectar

This one is too easy . . . and yet so much better than commercial.

1 can strawberry, apricot
  or peach nectar

paper cups
popsicle sticks

Pour into paper cups. Cover with foil. Make a small slit in center of foil cover. Insert popsicle stick and freeze.

Banana Frostee

Omit berries or peaches and substitute 3 dates and 1/4 cup cashews.

1/4 cup apple juice
2 bananas, sliced and frozen
1 tsp. vanilla

1/2 cup chilled fresh peaches
   or strawberries, chopped or sliced

   Combine juice and bananas in blender container. Blend until creamy. Quickly blend in chilled fruit. Serve immediately. Makes 2 servings.

Banapple Bars

1 cup pineapple juice
1 banana

paper cups
popsicle sticks

   Combine juice and banana in blender container. Blend on high speed until smooth. Fill cups. Cover with foil. Make slits in centers of foil covers. Insert popsicle sticks. Freeze.

Wiggle Sicles

You may substitute packaged gelatin or pudding for unflavored gelatin and fruit puree, but those products are high in sugar.

1 envelop unflavored gelatin
3/4 cup boiling water
1/2 cup fruit puree (strawberry, plum, peach, etc.)
paper cups
popsicle sticks

Dissolve gelatin in boiling water. Add fruit puree. Stir until well blended and pour into paper cups. Cover cups with foil. Make slits in centers of foil covers. Insert popsicle sticks in slits to keep them upright. Freeze. Peel off paper cup and eat.

Tropical Pops

Ask the kids what flavor it is . . .

1 apple, peeled and chopped
1 orange, peeled and sectioned
1 banana, peeled and sliced
1/2 cup fresh **or** canned pineapple

1 pear, peeled and chopped
1 cup frozen strawberries and juice
paper cups
popsicle sticks

Combine all ingredients in blender container and puree. Pour into paper cups. Cover with foil. Make slits in foil covers. Insert popsicle sticks. Freeze.

Hula Pops (page 96) ▶

Hawaiian Ice

Peaches can be substituted for nectarines.

4 nectarines, cubed
2 bananas
2 oranges
2 lemons
1 can (8 ozs.) crushed pineapple, with juice
1/2 cup water

Combine nectarines and banana in blender container. Blend until pureed. Squeeze juice from oranges and lemons and combine with fruit mixture. Add pineapple and water. Blend until smooth. Pour into a large container. Cover and freeze. When ready to serve, let stand at room temperature about 20 minutes. Scoop into individual dishes.

Squeezers

Homemade squeeze sticks are a lot healthier and cheaper than the store-bought ones, but you'll need the Seal-A-Meal apparatus to create them.

1 can (6 ozs.) frozen juice concentrate (orange, apple, grape or other)
8 large Seal-A-Meal bags
Seal-A-Meal apparatus

Prepare frozen concentrate (or any other fruit drink) according to directions on container. Fold bags into thirds and seal along folded edges. Cut open along one lengthwise edge and fill 3/4 full with fruit juice. Carefully seal open edges and place flat in freezer. When frozen, carefully cut into thirds along seal lines. Snip off one end, and let children squeeze out popsicle from bottom end.

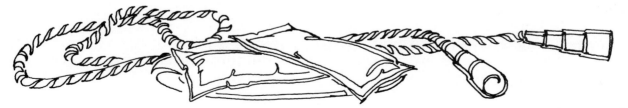

Frozen Wedgies

2 apples
1/2 cup peanut butter

1/4 cup coconut, sunflower seeds,
   granola **or** Rice Krispies

Cut apples into wedges and remove cores. Spread peanut butter on each wedge. Sprinkle with coconut or other toppings. Arrange on plates in a single layer. Freeze. Wrap in plastic wrap when frozen.

Frozen Bananas

Cut these into small chips for the young ones.

2 bananas
1/2 cup peanut butter

1/2 cup finely chopped peanuts, walnuts or wheat germ
4 popsicle sticks

Peel bananas and cut in half. Push a popsicle stick into each banana half. Wrap in plastic wrap and freeze. When frozen, dip into bowl of peanut butter and then into chopped nuts and serve.

Arctic Oranges

Save this one for a special occasion.

3 oranges
1/4 cup honey (or less, if desired)
1/2 cup water
1 tbs. lemon juice

Using a zigzag pattern, cut the tops off the oranges and hollow out the insides. Set oranges in muffin cups so they won't topple over. Squeeze and strain the juice. Set aside. Cook honey and water in small saucepan over low heat until slightly thickened, about 15 minutes. Add orange juice and lemon juice to the mixture. Fill oranges and freeze. For a festive look, top with yogurt and a cherry. (Mom, add 3 tablespoons of Gran Marnier to the mixture and serve it to your friends!)

Frozen Jammies

3 cups buttermilk   2 cups strawberry **or** plum jam

Beat ingredients together until blended. Pour into ice cube trays and freeze until firm. Release jammies from tray and beat with electric mixer until fluffy. Spoon into individual containers and return to freezer.

Fruit Sherbies

Never even *mention* the word buttermilk and they'll ask for more.

1 can (6 ozs.) frozen orange juice concentrate   2/3 cup buttermilk
3 cans water   paper cups
2 cups fruit puree **or** nectar   popsicle sticks

Combine ingredients. Pour into paper cups. Cover cups with foil. Make a small slit in center of cover. Insert popsicle stick. Freeze.

Gellapops

Much more nutritious than commercial popsicles.

1-1/2 packages unflavored gelatin
3/4 cup boiling water
1 can (6 ozs.) frozen juice concentrate (orange, apple, grape, etc.)
2 cups water
1 large container (32 ozs.) plain yogurt
popsicle molds **or** paper cups and popsicle sticks

Dissolve gelatin in boiling water in mixing bowl. Add juice and 2 cups water. Add yogurt and stir until blended. Pour into popsicle molds or paper cups. If using paper cups, cover cups with foil. Make a small slit in center of foil cover. Insert popsicle stick and freeze.

Cinnamon Sicles

Just like eating frozen apple pie.

1 cup plain yogurt
1 cup applesauce
1 tbs. honey (if desired)

1/2 tsp. cinnamon
paper cups
popsicle sticks

Blend yogurt, applesauce and honey. Pour into paper cups. Cover with foil. Make slit in center of oil and insert popsicle sticks. Freeze.

Frozen Yoggies

1 cup reconstituted frozen orange juice
2 cups (1 pint) plain yogart
1 tsp. vanilla

paper cups
popsicle sticks

Combine juice, yogurt and vanilla. Pour into paper cups. Cover with foil. Make slit in center of foil and insert popsicle stick. Freeze until firm.

Hawaiian Ice (page 88) ▶
Whole Wheat Brownies (page 59)

Hula Pops

1 cup plain yogurt
1 banana
1 tsp. honey (if desired)
1/2 cup orange **or** pineapple juice

1 cup strawberries, peaches, apricots,
   nectarines **or** pineapple
paper cups
popsicle sticks

Combine ingredients in blender container. Blend on high speed until smooth. Pour into paper cups. Cover cups with foil. Make a slit in center of cover. Insert stick. Freeze.

Peacheritos

Try strawberries or bananas, too.

1 can (28 ozs.) peaches **or** 3 ripe peaches   1-1/2 cups whole milk

Combine ingredients in blender container. Blend until smooth. Pour into paper cups. Cover cups with foil. Make a small slit in cover and insert popsicle sticks. Freeze.

Pizzazz Pops

1 cup Eagle Brand milk **or** half and half
1 bottle (28 ozs.) flavored soda
1/2 cup lemon juice

paper cups
popsicle sticks

Mix all ingredients well. Pour into paper cups. Cover cups with foil. Make a small slit in the centers of foil covers. Insert popsicle sticks. Freeze.

Banana Creamies

2 bananas
1/4 cup **each** pineapple and strawberries
1/2 cup heavy cream, whipped

paper cups
popsicle sticks

Place fruit in blender container. Blend until smooth. Fold into whipped cream. Spoon into paper cups. Cover cups with foil. Make a small slit in center of cover. Insert popsicle sticks. Freeze.

Chocksicles

1 cup plain yogurt
3 tbs. chocolate milk drink powder **or**
   2 tbs. cocoa and 1 tsp. honey

paper cups
popsicle sticks

Blend ingredients and pour into cups. Add sticks and freeze.

Rabbit Sherbet

It's devious but delicious and carrots are an important source of vitamins.

1 cup cooked carrots
1/4 cup orange juice

1 pint orange sherbet, softened

Combine carrots and orange juice in blender container. Blend until smooth. Fold into softened sherbet. Pour into a large plastic container or bowl. Cover and freeze. Serve scooped out into individual cups.

Puddin'wich

These are now sold commercially, but yours will be higher in nutrition.

1 cup plain yogurt
1/2 cup peanut butter

graham crackers, chocolate wafers
or oatmeal cookies

Combine yogurt and peanut butter. Spread onto graham crackers or cookies. Top with another cracker. Wrap in plastic wrap. Freeze.

Frozen Sandwich

1/2 cup vanilla ice milk, softened
1/4 cup peanut butter

4 peanut butter cookies
1/4 cup finely chopped peanuts

Mix softened ice milk with peanut butter. Refreeze until firm. Spread peanut butter-ice milk on two cookies. Top with remaining cookies. Roll edges in chopped nuts. Makes 2 servings.

Tricks to "Smuggling" Good Things Into Every Meal

BETTER BREAKFASTS

Are you stuck in the bacon-and-egg or cereal rut? Take a look at the recipes in this chapter and you'll see that your dilemma is over. There are so many wonderful alternatives that children love. Who says you have to eat those "regular old breakfast things" anyway?

Now you can be creative and provide a wholesome breakfast in minutes. Most of the recipes offer a complete meal, and can be made the evening before or on weekends and frozen. All you have to do on those rushed, early mornings is heat the treat-of-the-day in a microwave or conventional oven or in the toaster. You can mix and match with recipes from other chapters in the book, for more variety.

Hot Cereal Surprise

Mikey won't eat his Maypo? How about this little surprise . . .

1 cup cooked oatmeal, cream of wheat **or** rice
1 chopped apple
1 cup milk
1 to 2 tbs. honey (if desired)
1/4 cup raisins, apricots **or** dates
1/4 tsp. cinnamon

Combine cooked cereal, apple, milk, honey, fruit and cinnamon in a saucepan. Cook over low heat 5 to 10 minutes. Serve hot.

Egg in a Basket (page 109) ▶

Bacon-Butter Breakfast

Kids really love this high-protein breakfast.

1 slice whole grain bread
1 tsp. mayonnaise
1 tbs. peanut butter
1 slice cooked bacon

Toast bread and spread with mayonnaise. Spread peanut butter over mayonnaise and crumble bacon over top. Serve open-faced, cut up into triangles. Makes 1 serving.

Breakfast Spread

Maybe little appetites just need a change from bacon, eggs and toast.

2 hard-cooked eggs, finely chopped
2 tbs. mayonnaise
4 slices bacon, cooked and crumbled
1/4 tsp. Worcestershire sauce (if desired)
rye crackers **or** whole wheat bread

Mix eggs, mayonnaise, bacon and Worcestershire together until good spreading consistency. Serve on crackers or bread.

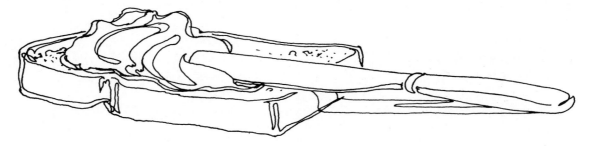

Cottage Eggs

Add a little more flavor and a lot more protein.

4 eggs   1/2 cup cottage cheese

Beat eggs in a bowl. Add cottage cheese. Scramble in non-stick skillet until light and fluffy. Makes 2 to 4 servings.

Scrambled Bread

In a hurry? Here's a great breakfast cooked in one pan.

1 tsp butter or margarine   2 eggs, beaten
1 slice whole wheat bread,   2 slices cooked bacon,
  broken into small pieces   coarsely crumbled

Melt butter in frying pan. Add bread and saute until golden brown. Add remaining ingredients and scramble until fluffy.

UFO's

Cook toast and egg together and you've got an unidentified frying object.

1 tbs. butter or margarine
1 slice whole wheat bread
1 egg (may be scrambled if desired)

Melt half of butter in skillet. Spread the rest on one side of bread. Cut a hole in the center of the bread with a cookie cutter. Fry slice of bread with buttered side up in skillet until browned. Turn bread over and break egg into center of hole. Cook until egg starts to set. Turn again to cook the other side of egg. Serve immediately. Makes 1 serving.

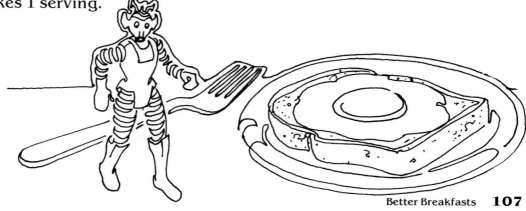

Breakfast Burros

Fun to eat. The warm eggs melt the cheese.

1 flour tortilla
2 eggs, scrambled

1/4 cup grated Cheddar cheese,
or Swiss **or** Jack

Warm tortilla in non-stick skillet. Top tortilla with scrambled eggs and sprinkle with cheese. Fold and serve. Makes one serving.

Swiss Omelet

A tasty way to enhance "plain old" eggs. Serve with whole wheat toast.

2 eggs
1 apple, peeled, cored and chopped

1/4 cup grated Swiss cheese

Mix ingredients in a bowl. Scramble in non-stick skillet until cooked and fluffy. Serve immediately.

Egg In A Basket

Sprinkle cheese on top just before serving.

1 unbaked biscuit per serving
1 egg per serving

Cheddar cheese

Place biscuits in muffin tin, shaping to fit sides and leaving a well. Break eggs into "baskets." Bake in 400°F. oven 10 to 15 minutes.

Macaroni Omelet

Serve in scooped out orange halves for a fresh look.

2 eggs, beaten
1 cup cooked broccoli, chopped

1/2 cup cooked macaroni
1/4 cup Parmesan cheese

Mix eggs with broccoli and macaroni. Scramble in non-stick skillet until fluffy. Serve sprinkled with Parmesan cheese.

Bacon 'N' Egg Sandwiches

Great for a breakfast "on the go."

1 can (8 ozs.) refrigerator crescent rolls
4 ozs. sliced Cheddar cheese
8 slices bacon, cooked, drained and crumbled
1/2 cup milk
2 eggs

Separate crescent dough into triangles. Lay half the triangles on an un-greased cookie sheet with sides or a shallow baking pan. Pinch up edges to form rims on triangles. Place cheese slices over dough and trim to fit. Sprinkle bacon over cheese. Mix milk and eggs and spoon into triangle shells. Top with remaining dough triangles but do not seal. Bake at 350°F. for 35 minutes. Makes 4 servings.

Shark Eggs

A hearty egg dish that will get them through two recesses.

6 hard-cooked eggs
1 small can (4 ozs.) tuna, drained
2 green onions, chopped (if desired)
3 heaping tbs. mayonnaise
dash paprika

Slice eggs in half. Scoop yolks out into mixing bowl. Add tuna and break up with a fork. Stir in onions and mayonnaise until blended. Fill egg whites with mixture. Sprinkle with paprika.

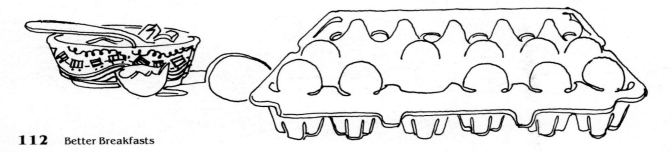

Stuffed Eggs

Children love stuffed eggs because they can eat them with their fingers. Many "good things" can be mixed into the yolks. Here are three suggestions.

4 hard-cooked eggs, shelled

Slice eggs in half lengthwise and scoop out yolks. Mix yolks with one of the following combinations. Fill whites with mixture. Refrigerate. Makes 4 servings.

1 oz. cream cheese
1 tbs. sour cream
1 tsp. finely minced parsley, thyme
   or other fresh herbs

1/2 cup chopped cooked ham
1 tbs. melted margarine
1/4 tsp. paprika

1 tbs. mayonnaise
1 tsp. mustard
1 tsp. diced pickles or relish

Cheese Toast

Simple to make and high in protein—plus a nice change!

2 tbs. water
2 cups grated Cheddar, Longhorn, Jack **or** Swiss cheese
1 egg, beaten
4 slices bread or toast

Bring water to boil in frying pan and add cheese. Stir until cheese is melted. Stir in egg and cook until white sets. Serve spread on bread or toast. Makes 4 servings.

Note: You might consider switching to some of the light cheeses that are made with skim milk instead of whole milk. They have 1/3 the cholesterol and a lot less fat. They come in all flavors—American, Cheddar, Swiss and Jack.

Nutty Fruity Toast

How to put a whole breakfast on a slice of toast.

1/4 cup peanut butter
1/4 cup chopped raisins **or** dried apricots
1 tbs. jam or preserves
1 tsp. cinnamon
4 slices whole wheat bread
1 egg
1/4 cup milk
1 tbs. butter

Combine peanut butter, raisins, jam and cinnamon. Spread on two slices of bread. Top with remaining bread. Beat eggs and stir in milk. Dip each sandwich in mixture. Melt butter in skillet. Brown sandwiches on both sides. Makes 2 sandwiches.

Square Meal Squares

Here's another complete-meal-on-toast.

1 cup cottage cheese
1 tbs. honey (if desired)
1/2 cup chopped walnuts
2 slices whole wheat toast **or** waffle squares
1 banana, sliced
2 tsp. wheat germ

Combine cottage cheese, honey and nuts. Spread on toast or waffle. Top with banana slices and sprinkle with wheat germ. Makes 2 servings.

Sweetbread

This will make a "breakfast eater" out of everyone. Prepare the mix the night before so it will be ready to use in the morning when you don't have much time.

1 cup cottage cheese
1/4 cup chopped dates **or** prunes
1/4 cup nuts and sunflower seeds
1 tsp. honey (if desired)
1/2 tsp. cinnamon
2 slices wheat bread **or** English muffin

Mix cheese, fruit, nuts and seasonings together. Store in refrigerator. When ready to serve, spread on bread slices or muffin halves. Broil until bubbly. Makes 2 servings.

Fruit 'N' Cheese Toast

A wholesome American version of a Danish sweet roll.

1 tbs. butter
2 eggs
1 tbs. milk
2 slices bread
1 oz. cream cheese, softened
1 small apple, pear **or** banana, chopped
1/4 tsp. lemon juice
2 tbs. raisins

Melt butter in a small shallow baking pan in a 450°F. oven. Spread butter evenly in pan. Separate one egg. Beat 1 whole egg and 1 egg white with milk. Dip bread in egg mixture, coating both sides. Place in buttered pan. Bake 5 minutes at 450°F. Beat cream cheese and remaining yolk together. Mix fruit, lemon juice and raisins. Remove bread from oven. Spread each slice with cheese mixture. Top with fruit. Bake 5 minutes longer. Serve warm.

Instant Brunch (page 122) ▶

Coconut Toasties

For a special birthday breakfast surprise.

2 eggs
1/2 cup milk
1/2 cup crushed corn flakes
1/2 cup coconut
2 tbs. margarine
8 slices whole wheat bread
1 can (8 ozs.) crushed pineapple, warmed

Beat eggs with milk in pie plate. Set aside. Combine corn flakes and coconut in another pie plate or shallow bowl. Heat margarine on griddle over midium heat. Dip each slice of bread into egg mixture and then into coconut mixture, coating both sides. Cook on griddle until browned on both sides. Serve with pineapple topping. Makes 4 servings.

Make-Believe Waffles

Whole wheat bread makes good "waffles," but this recipe will taste even better if you have time to make real waffles, using part whole wheat flour. Keep handy in the freezer for snacks, too. Cut them into smaller squares and serve with cheese or other spreads.

1 egg
1/4 cup milk
1 tbs. melted margarine
2 tbs. grated Parmesan **or** Romano cheese
2 slices whole wheat bread

Heat the waffle iron. Combine egg, milk, margarine and cheese in a pie plate or shallow bowl. Dip bread slices into mixture, one at a time, until well coated. Bake in waffle iron until golden brown. This recipe needs no topping if you use Parmesan cheese to flavor it.

Instant Brunch

It's fun to eat as a sandwich and so delicious, they won't know it's good for them. If you make your own waffles, use part whole wheat flour and add up to one-half cup of wheat germ. Make extras and freeze them.

2 heaping tbs. cream cheese
2 tbs. strawberry jam
2 heaping tbs. finely chopped walnuts
2 waffles, toasted

Mix cheese, jam and walnuts. Spread on tasted waffle. Cover with second waffle. Cut into quarters and serve.

Banana Francais

Fortified French toast.

2 eggs
1 banana, peeled and chopped
1/4 cup milk
1/2 tsp. cinnamon
2 tsp. corn oil
4 slices whole wheat bread

Combine eggs, banana, milk and cinnamon in blender container. Blend until smooth. Pour into pie plate. Soak bread in banana mixture. Heat 1 teaspoon oil in large frying pan until hot. Place bread in hot frying pan. Spoon a teaspoon of banana mixture over each slice of bread. Cook over medium-high heat until brown on both sides.

Pot Pourri Pancakes

Try substituting other vegetables. Remember, French toast and pancakes freeze well so keep them on hand to pop into the toaster when needed.

2 eggs, separated
1-1/2 tsp. salt
1 tbs. honey (if desired)
1 cup milk
1 cup whole wheat flour
1/2 cup shredded carrots
1 cup finely chopped celery

Mix egg yolks with salt, honey, milk and flour. Beat well to blend. Add vegetables. Beat egg whites until stiff and fold into batter. Spoon onto griddle and bake on both sides, turning when bubbles form.

Funny Face Pancakes

When you are frying the pancakes, fill a large medicine dropper with batter and make a face: first the eyes, nose and mouth—letting them cook for a few seconds. Then pour more batter over the facial features and turn when brown on first side.

3 eggs
1 cup cottage cheese
1/4 cup flour
dash salt (if desired)

Beat eggs well. Add cottage cheese and beat again. Add flour and salt and mix well. Fry in non-stick or lighty oiled skillet.

Funnel Cakes

An old favorite, a new package . . .

1 cup **plus** 2 tbs. flour
1 tsp. baking powder
dash salt
3/4 cup milk
1 egg, beaten
funnel

Beat ingredients together well. Lightly grease a frying pan and heat for several minutes. Pour 1/4 cup of batter into a funnel (don't forget to put your finger over the end!). Over hot pan, release finger and let batter run out in a stream, while you make a spiral design with funnel. Fry 6 to 8 minutes, until golden brown, turning once, gently. Repeat with remaining batter. Drain on paper towels and serve hot or cold.

Funnel Cakes (page 126) ▶

Picky-Eater Pancakes

Pour the batter out onto a hot pan or griddle in a free form manner and cook. After serving, have your child guess what you made. Whatever he or she guesses, of course, is right!

1 small zucchini	**OR**	1 small zucchini
1-1/2 cups flour		1 cup pancake mix
3 tsp. baking powder		1/4 cup milk
1/2 tsp. salt (if desired)		1 egg
1 egg, beaten		
1 cup milk		
2 tbs. oil		

Steam zucchini and puree in blender. Mix with remaining ingredients. Stir only until mixed. Cook pancakes, turning only once. Serve with Pancake Toppings on page 129.

Pancake Toppings

Applesauce
Frozen berries, thawed and stirred or blended
Cream cheese
Flavored yogurt
Jam or preserves
Warm honey
Melted peanut butter (thin with apple juice, if desired)
Fresh fruit puree
Cottage cheese
Melted cheese
Cream cheese and fruit
Spiced pineapple: 1/4 cup crushed pineapple blended with 1 teaspoon vanilla and 1/4 teaspoon cinnamon
Combinations of any of the above.

Blintz Souffle

For a special birthday breakfast. Buy the frozen blintzes at your supermarket.

2 tbs. butter or margarine
6 frozen blintzes, defrosted
2 eggs

3/4 cup sour cream
1/4 tsp. vanilla
1 tbs. orange juice

Melt butter in 8- by 8-inch pan. Add blintzes. Blend remaining ingredients and pour over blintzes. Bake at 350°F. for 40 minutes. Serve immediately. Makes 6 servings.

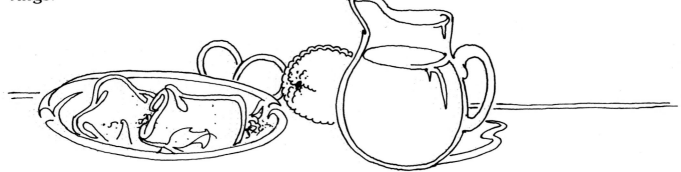

Fruit and Cereal Squares

For a breakfast-on-the-run.

3 cups whole wheat flour
2 tsp. baking powder
1/4 tsp. salt
3 cups quick oats
1/4 cup honey
1-1/2 cups margarine
2 cups jam or fruit puree

Combine first five ingredients. Cut in margarine until crumbly. Pat 2/3 of mixture on bottom of ungreased jellyroll pan (10- by 18-inches). Spread with jam and sprinkle remaining ingredients over top. Bake at 350°F. for 30 minutes until lightly browned.

Breakfast Bars

A complete breakfast—wheat, fruit, milk and high in protein.

2-1/2 cups all bran **or** granola cereal **or** rolled oats
3/4 cup flour
1 tsp. baking powder
1/4 tsp. salt (optional)
1/4 cup honey (or less)
1 banana, mashed
1/2 cup melted margarine
1 egg
1 tsp. vanilla

Set one-half cup cereal aside. Combine remaining ingredients. Spread into greased 11 by 7-inch baking dish. Crush reserved cereal and sprinkle over batter. Bake 350°F. for 25 minutes. Cool a few minutes and cut into squares.

Easy Cinnamon Rolls

A sugarless way to make cinnamon rolls.

1 loaf frozen bread dough, thawed
1/4 cup softened butter
2 tbs. cinnamon
1 apple, chopped
1 cup raisins
1/2 cup pecans (if desired)

Roll dough into 9 by 12-inch rectangle. Spread with butter and sprinkle with cinnamon. Spread chopped apple and raisins over dough. Roll up like jelly roll. Cut into 1-inch slices. Place on greased cookie sheet and let rise until nearly double in size. Bake at 350°F. for 25 to 35 minutes or until brown and done. Makes 1 dozen.

LIVELY LUNCHES

Whether you have a preschooler who still has lunch at home or an older child who takes lunch to school, adding variety, excitement and a little color to his or her food will get results you won't believe.

It takes only minutes to prepare something delicious and nutritious if you plan ahead and have the ingredients on hand. Every lunch can be something your child looks forward to. Try different combinations from various recipes in this chapter for more variety. Select a snack from Super Snacks to add to the lunch box fixings and complete the meal with one of the Dynamite Drinks for the thermos.

Make every lunch as special as you can to stimulate the desire to eat and try new things. Even if your little one doesn't go to school, occasionally pack lunch in a lunch box and see how it increases his or her interest in eating.

Tuna Boats

Add seeds, shredded carrots, chopped celery or relish to tuna mixture for an added attraction. Cheddar cheese, or fat carrots thinly sliced lengthwise, cut into triangles make neat sails.

1 can (6-1/2 to 7 ozs.) tuna, drained
2 heaping tbs. mayonnaise
1 small green pepper

Mix tuna with mayonnaise and any other desired ingredients. Cut green pepper in half or quarters (for a small child), lengthwise. Remove seeds and membranes. Fill with tuna mixture. Add sails, if desired. Makes 1 to 2 servings.

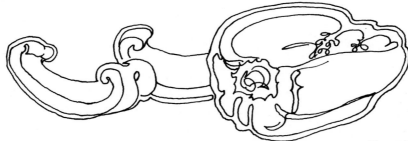

Tuna Boats (page 136) ▶

Mama Mia Cubes

These are best when served cold. Remove picks if serving to small children, or replace them with pretzel sticks just before serving.

8 thin slices baked or boiled ham
1 medium-size cantaloupe

Pretzel sticks **or** toothpicks

Cut ham into 1-inch wide strips. Cut cantaloupe into cubes. Wrap a ham strip around each cantaloupe cube and secure with toothpicks. Chill and serve.

Tomato Balloons

1 tomato
1/4 cup cottage cheese

1/4 cup tuna

Cut stem off tomato and scoop out insides. Mix cheese and tuna. Stuff into tomato. Makes 1 serving.

"Add To" Suggestions

Peanut Butter, egg salad and tuna salad are excellent bases for adding extra nutrition to a child's diet. Following are a few suggestions.

To Peanut Butter add:
- hard-cooked egg, chopped
- raisins
- chopped banana
- shredded carrot
- chopped apple
- crushed pineapple
- grated cheese
- 1 tbs. **each** per serving:
  - sesame seed and celery
  - raisins and sunflower seed
  - chopped nuts and coconut
- chopped pears

To Egg Salad add:
- sliced olives
- chopped sardines
- diced celery
- diced ham
- sunflower seeds
- crumbled bacon

To Tuna Salad add:
- chopped egg
- chopped apple
- diced celery
- cubed cream cheese and pineapple
- chopped walnuts
- bean sprouts

Pinwheels

Make these ahead of time and use as needed.

1 package (3 ozs.) cream cheese, softened
1 tsp. Worcestershire sauce
1/2 tsp. chopped chives

1/4 tsp. powdered mustard
6 thin slices boiled ham
rye bread rounds

Blend cheese, Worcestershire sauce, chives and mustard. Spread over ham slices and roll up, jelly roll-fashion. Chill and cut into slices. Serve with rye bread. Makes 2 to 3 servings.

Peanut Butter Pinwheels

2 slices whole wheat bread
1/4 cup peanut butter

1 can (3 ozs.) deviled ham

Flatten bread with a rolling pin. Mix peanut butter and deviled ham. Spread onto bread. Roll up like a jelly roll and cut into slices.

Bubble And Squeal

Kids really like this high-protein spread. Serve on wheat crackers or toast.

2 hard-cooked eggs, chopped
1/2 cup chopped walnuts

1 cup grated Cheddar cheese
3 tbs. mayonnaise

Mix all ingredients together well. Spread on crackers or toasted bread rounds. Broil to melt cheese or serve cold without melting cheese.

Nut Cracker

Also, serve this cream cheese-pineapple mixture with carrot sticks and pear slices for dipping.

1 package (3 ozs.) cream cheese
1/4 cup crushed pineapple, well drained

1/4 cup chopped pecans
whole wheat crackers

Mix cheese, pineapple and pecans. Spread on wheat crackers. Makes 1 cup.

Applesauce Toasties

Try ricotta cheese if someone in your group isn't fond of cottage cheese.

1/4 cup peanut butter
1/4 cup applesauce
2 dried apricots, chopped

1/4 cup cottage cheese
4 slices whole wheat toast

Mix peanut butter, applesauce, apricots and cottage cheese. Spread on two toast slices. Top with remaining slices of toast. Makes 2 sandwiches.

Ban-Nutter-Butter Sandwich

1/4 cup peanut butter
4 slices whole wheat bread
1 banana, sliced

Spread peanut butter on two slices of bread. Lay banana slices on top of peanut butter. Cover with remaining bread. Makes 2 sandwiches.

Rabbit Butter

You can hide just about anything in "good old" peanut butter.

1/2 cup peanut butter
1/4 cup shredded carrots

4 slices whole wheat bread

Mix peanut butter with carrots. Spread on 2 slices of bread. Top with remaining slices. Makes 2 sandwiches.

Strawberry 'N' Cream Sandwich

Substitute frozen fruit for preserves if you like.

1/4 cup cream cheese, softened
2 tbs. strawberry preserves

1 tbs. wheat germ
2 slices whole wheat bread

Stir cheese, preserves and wheat germ together. Spread on bread slice. Top with remaining bread. Cut in half or quarters and serve. Makes one sandwich.

Apple Pie Sandwich

Fruit and vegetables, high in protein—and it still tastes like dessert.

1/4 cup cream cheese
2 tbs. chopped walnuts
2 tbs. chopped celery

3 tbs. chopped apple
1 tsp. cinnamon
4 slices raisin bread

Mix cream cheese, walnuts, celery, apple and cinnamon. Spread on two slices of raisin bread. Top with remaining bread slices. Makes 2 sandwiches.

Thanksgiving Sandwich

1/2 cup chopped turkey meat
2 to 3 tbs. cream cheese

2 tbs. cranberry sauce
4 slices whole wheat bread

Mix turkey with cheese and cranberry sauce. Spread on two slices of bread. Top with remaining slices. Makes 2 sandwiches.

◀ **Bahama Bagels (page 150)**

Fancy Ham Sandwich

2 drops food coloring
1 tbs. milk
4 slices wheat bread

1 can (3 ozs.) deviled ham spread
2 tbs. mayonnaise
1/4 cup cooked peas, mashed

Mix food coloring with milk and lightly paint a design on two slices of bread. Toast all four slices lightly. Mix peas with ham spread and mayonnaise. Spread plain toast slices and top with decorated slices. Makes 2 sandwiches.

Nutwich

1/2 cup raisins
1 package (3 ozs.) cream cheese
1/2 cup peanut butter

1 tsp. honey (if desired)
1/4 cup chopped walnuts
4 slices nut, banana **or** apricot bread

Soak raisins in hot water 10 minutes. Drain and chop. Combine with cream cheese, peanut butter, honey and walnuts. Spread between slices of bread.

Piranha Pita Pocket

Substitute tuna for sardines, if desired.

4 sardines, chopped
2 tbs. sweet pickle relish
2 tbs. mayonnaise
1/4 cup shredded Jack cheese
2 small pita bread pockets

Mix sardines, relish, mayonnaise and cheese. Spoon mixture into pita pockets.

Pocket Surprise!

You guessed it! Fill a pita pocket with last night's spaghetti dinner, tuna casserole or anything that your child likes! Send along some carrot or celery sticks and green pepper pieces for crunch.

Ham And Cheese Pillows

Substitute deviled chicken for ham and add a little celery.

1 can (3 ozs.) deviled ham
2 tbs. mayonnaise

1/4 cup shredded Jack cheese
2 small pita bread pockets

Mix ham, mayonnaise and cheese. Spoon into pita pockets.

"Ruffage" Stuffer

1/4 cup bean sprouts
1/4 cup combination of chopped celery, carrot, green pepper and mushrooms
1 to 2 tbs. ranch-style **or** thousand island dressing
pita bread

Combine bean sprouts and chopped vegetables in medium bowl. Add dressing to moisten. Stuff into small pita pocket. Makes 1 to 2 servings.

Mozzarella Muffins

French bread or rye rounds make good substitutes for English muffins.

1/4 cup mozzarella cheese   2 English muffins, sliced
2 tbs. mayonnaise

Mix cheese with mayonnaise and spread on muffin halves. Broil until cheese is bubbly.

New England Muffins

Stick two together and tuck into the lunchbox.

1/4 cup shredded Cheddar cheese   2 English muffins
1/4 cup shredded apple

Sprinkle cheese and apples on muffin halves. Broil until bubbly or bake at 350°F. for 10 minutes.

Pizza Gobbler

For variety, use any topping your child likes.

1/2 cup pizza sauce
4 English muffins, sliced

1/4 cup Mozzarella **or** Jack cheese
1 turkey frank, sliced

Spread sauce on muffins. Sprinkle with cheese and top with hot dog slices. Broil until cheese is bubbly.

Bahama Bagels

A nice change for the brown-bagger.

1/2 cup cream cheese
1/4 tbs. crushed pineapple

1/4 tbs. chopped walnuts
2 bagels, sliced in half

Mix cheese, pineapple and nuts. Spread between bagel slices.

Nacho Sandwich

2 flour tortillas
1/2 cup refried beans
1/4 cup shredded Cheddar cheese

1/4 cup shredded lettuce
1/4 cup chopped tomato
2 tbs. sour cream

Fill flour tortillas with ingredients in order given. Fold over one end of each tortilla and roll up. Makes 2 sandwiches.

Cheese Pups

1 can (8 ozs.) refrigerator crescent rolls
4 turkey franks
4 strips American cheese (1/2 by 3 inches)

4 wooden skewers
2 tbs. barbeque sauce
1/4 cup bread crumbs

Separate dough into 4 rectangles. Cut a slit down length of each frank and insert cheese. Push skewers into one end of each frank. Wrap franks in dough and pinch edges and ends to seal. Brush with sauce and dip in crumbs. Place on greased cookie sheet. Bake at 400°F. for 20 minutes. Makes 4 servings.

Ham 'N' Cheese Pop-Ups

1 cup chopped, cooked ham
2 tbs. margarine, softened
1 tbs. mayonnaise

1 tsp. prepared mustard
1 can (8 ozs.) refrigerator-type biscuits
4 slices American **or** Cheddar cheese

Combine ham, margarine, mayonnaise and mustard. Press half of biscuits into cupcake tins, making a well in each. Spoon half of ham mixture into biscuit cups. Top with a cheese slice. Cover with remaining ham mixture. Top with another biscuit, flattened to fit. Do not seal. Bake at 350°F. 15 to 20 minutes.

Mermaid Pillows

1 package (10 ozs.) cornbread mix
1 can (6-1/2 ozs.) tuna packed in water, drained

1 tbs. dehydrated minced onion
1/4 cup chopped olives

Prepare cornbread according to package directions. Stir in tuna and onion. Pour into greased 10- by 15-inch jellyroll pan. Scatter olives over top. Bake at 400°F. for 15 to 20 minutes. Cut into small squares.

Nacho Sandwich (page 151) ▶

Chinese Chicken Puffs

Children will eat many different things if they come dressed this way. The puffs are easy to make. Double the recipe and freeze the extras.

Cream Puffs:
  1/2 cup water
  1/4 cup butter **or** margarine
  1/2 cup flour
  dash salt
  2 eggs

Filling:
  1/2 cup chopped cooked chicken
  2 tbs. mayonnaise
  2 to 3 tbs. drained crushed pineapple
  1/4 cup Chinese noodles

Heat water and butter to a rolling boil in saucepan. Stir in all of the flour and salt. Stir vigorously over low heat until mixture leaves the sides of pan and forms a ball. Remove from heat. Beat eggs in thoroughly, one at a time. Beat mixture until smooth and velvety. Drop by tablespoonfuls onto ungreased baking sheet, 3 inches apart. Bake at 450°F. for 15 minutes. Reduce heat to 325°F. and bake 25 minutes. Remove puffs from oven and split in half. Turn oven off and return puffs to oven to dry, about 20 minutes. Cool on rack. Makes 4 puffs. To make filling, mix chicken, mayonnaise, pineapple and noodles. Chill. Just before serving fill puffs.

Charlie's Choice

1 can (6 ozs.) tuna, drained
2 hard-cooked eggs, chopped
1 cup cooked macaroni

3 tbs. mayonnaise
4 medium size cream puff shells
　(see page 154)

Combine tuna, eggs, macaroni and mayonnaise. Spoon into cream puff shells. Serve immediately. Makes 4 servings.

Kingfish Stuffing

Any filling tastes twice as good served in a cream puff shell (see page 154).

1 can (6 ozs.) tuna, drained
2 tbs. mayonnaise
1 tbs. chopped apple

1 tbs. grated carrot
1 tbs. raisins
4 medium size cream puff shells

Combine tuna, mayonnaise, apple, carrot and raisins. Fill cream puff shells with mixture. Serve immediately. Makes 4 servings.

Popovers

Another way to package a lunch that fascinates children. Popovers lend themselves to any kind of spread and they temp a child to try something different. Serve hot.

1 cup flour
1/2 tsp. salt

1 cup milk
2 eggs

Beat ingredients together with rotary beater just until smooth. Pour into well buttered muffin tins (3/4 full) or large custard cups (1/2 full). Bake in 425°F. oven until golden brown, 40 to 45 minutes. Serve immediately filled with desired filling. Makes about 6 popovers.

Popover Partners

All-American Special

1/2 cup peanut butter
1/4 cup grated cheese
1/4 cup ricotta cheese
1 tbs. honey
1 tsp. cinnamon

Mix ingredients together until blended. Enough filling for 2 to 4 popovers.

Scrapple

1/4 cup apple butter
1/4 cup shredded Cheddar cheese

Mix ingredients together until blended. Enough spread for 2 to 4 popovers.

DASHING DINNERS

There is a way to help your child become more interested in trying new dishes. Make them more interesting and serve with a flair. (No one has to know that tucked into an old favorite is a food usually left untouched.) If spaghetti is a favorite, sneak a little tuna or zucchini into the sauce. Introduce it by talking about Italy and the little boys and girls who live there. This gives the new dish a special image, and your child not only learns about new foods but also about new places and people. Who could resist trying something with all that going for it? Try this idea anytime the name or origin of the recipe allows. There are lots of possibilities for imagination in this chapter—Cowboy Leather, Mr. MacGregor's Cabbage, Peter Cottontails and Popeye's Burgers, to name just a few.

Veggie Dips

Dips are a fun way to get kids to eat vegetables. Served with dinner they are both salad and vegetable.

Vegetables to use:
   carrot sticks
   celery sticks
   green pepper sticks
   cherry tomatoes
   zucchini wheels
   cucumber wheels
   broccoli pieces
   caulifloweretes

Dutchbelt Dip - Combine:
   1 cup plain yogurt
   1 cup cottage cheese
   1/4 cup Parmesan cheese

Bacon Cheese Dip - Combine:
   8 ounces American cheese, melted
   4 strips cooked bacon, crumbled
   1tsp. mustard

Kermit's Dip - Combine:
   1 avocado, mashed
   2 tbs mayonnaise
   2 tsp. lemon juice

Devil Dip - Combine:
   3 hard-cooked eggs, mashed
   2 tbs. mayonnaise
   2 tsp. mustard

Peter Cottontail (page 162)
Petite Apple Tart (page 184) ▶
Popeye Burger (page 178)

Peter Cottontails

The kids can help you make these.

1 package (3-ozs.) cream cheese **or** Cheddar cheese spread
1/2 cup shredded mild Cheddar **or** Jack cheese
1 cup finely shredded carrots
1/2 cup finely chopped walnuts **or** Grapenuts

   Beat cheeses together until blended. Stir in carrots. Cover and chill. Shape into balls. Roll in nuts or cereal and chill until ready to serve.

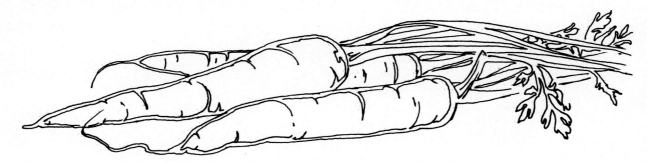

Mystery Gelatin

A very subversive way to sneak in the enemy.

1/2 cup cooked vegetables (beets, carrots, zucchini **or** other)
1 package (3 ozs.) strawberry **or** raspberry gelatin
1 cup boiling water
1/2 cup cold water
2 cups fresh fruit (strawberries, bananas, orange slices, peaches)

Puree vegetables in blender container. In mixing bowl dissolve gelatin in boiling water. Stir in cold water and pureed vegetables. Chill mixture until slightly thickened. Stir in fruit. Pour into large mold or individual molds. Chill until set. Makes 6 servings.

Spaghetti Salad

An Italian way of serving vegetables. Top with grated Parmesan cheese if desired. Use whole wheat or vegetable spaghetti for variety.

1 cup plain yogurt
1/2 cup mayonnaise
1 tsp. Italian seasoning herbs
1/2 pound spaghetti, cooked and well drained
1/2 cup chopped celery
2 tbs. chopped onion (if desired)
2 cups any combination sliced cooked carrots, zucchini, green beans,
    chopped cheese, green pepper strips, chopped hard-cooked eggs, flaked tuna
    or other favorites

Mix yogurt, mayonnaise and seasoning together well. Combine remaining ingredients in large mixing bowl. Toss with dressing. Chill before serving. Makes 4 to 6 servings.

Baked Veggie Spread

Serve with dinner or as an appetizer or snack.

1 eggplant, unpeeled
2 carrots
1 package (10 ozs.) French-cut green beans
3 small zucchini
3/4 cup catsup
1 can (8 ozs.) tomato sauce
1 tbs. oil

Chop all vegetables and place in baking dish. Combine catsup, sauce and oil. Pour over veggies. Bake, covered, at 325°F. for 1-1/2 hours. Serve cold as a spread with bread, rye or other crackers.

Corny Pudding

An unusual way to serve the evening vegetable.

2 eggs
1 cup water
1 can (16 ozs.) whole kernel corn
1 cup dates, finely chopped

Separate eggs and lightly beat yolks in mixing bowl. Add water and stir to blend. Place corn and dates in saucepan. Stir in yolk mixture. Cook over low heat for 15 minutes. Pour into blender container. Blend on high speed until smooth. Return to saucepan and cook 10 minutes, stirring constantly. Pour into mixing bowl and cool in refrigerator. When cool, beat egg whites until stiff and fold into mixture. Pour into individual serving dishes and chill. Makes 4 servings.

Note: Most of the major companies are offering canned vegetables without added salt. Some say ''natural pack'' and others say ''diet.'' If you buy regular canned vegetables, rinse them first to remove excess salt.

Mr. MacGregor's Cabbage

If your little Peter Rabbit hates cabbage, try this. The whole family will enjoy it.

1 pound cabbage shredded
White sauce:
   2 tbs. butter
   2 tbs. flour
   1 cup milk
dash nutmeg
1 cup chopped peanuts
1 cup grated Cheddar cheese

Steam cabbage just until crisp-tender. Make white sauce: melt butter over low heat. Remove from heat and blend in flour until smooth. Gradually add milk, stirring constantly. Cook over medium heat until sauce thickens and boils. Simmer at reduced heat, stirring, for 2 minutes to remove raw taste. Season with nutmeg. Arrange layers of cabbage, sauce, nuts and cheese in buttered casserole dish. Bake at 425°F. for 15 minutes. Makes 4 servings.

I-Hate-Vegetables Casserole

Bacon helps disguise the vegetables. Serve with a molded fruit salad and bread sticks.

12 slices bacon
1-1/2 cups croutons
1 pound fresh **or** frozen vegetable (asparagus, carrots, potatoes,
    green beans, cabbage **or** broccoli)
4 hard-cooked eggs, sliced
1 cup white sauce (see page 167)
1/2 cup Parmesan cheese

Fry bacon, drain well on paper towels and crumble. Arrange croutons, vegetables, 3/4 of crumbled bacon and eggs in layers in 9- by 9-inch baking dish. Top with sauce and sprinkle on cheese and remaining bacon. Bake at 375°F. until bubbly, about 45 minutes.

Popeye's Pie

This was the one that made a spinach lover out of Popeye.

1 pound fresh spinach, steamed **or** frozen spinach, thawed
1 egg
1/3 cup wheat germ
1/4 cup shredded Swiss **or** Cheddar cheese
1 tsp. Worcestershire sauce
pinch garlic powder
9-inch unbaked pie shell

Combine spinach, egg, wheat germ, cheese and seasonings. Pour into pie shell. Bake 400°F. for 25 minutes.

Eat Your Spinach

Substitute broccoli for spinach or try another vegetable.

1 package (10 ozs.) frozen, chopped spinach
1 package (3 ozs.) cream cheese, softened
1/4 cup butter **or** margarine, melted
1/2 cup toasted bread cubes **or** croutons
1/4 cup Parmesan cheese

Cook spinach according to package directions. Drain well. Mix spinach, cream cheese and half of the melted butter. Place in casserole. Mix stuffing and remaining butter. Sprinkle over top of spinach mixture. Bake at 350°F. for 30 minutes. Makes 4 servings.

Skinny Dips

My son could eat these every night! Now he helps me prepare them.

4 large potatoes, baked
1/2 cup shredded Cheddar cheese
4 strips bacon, cooked and crumbled
1 green onion, chopped (if desired)
1/2 cup buttermilk **or** blue cheese dressing

Cut potatoes in half lengthwise. Scoop out most of potato. Sprinkle cheese, bacon and green onion over skins. Heat in 350°F. oven 4 to 5 minutes, until cheese is bubbly. Serve with dressing. Makes 4 servings.

Mexican Skinny Dips—Sprinkle potato skins with Jack **and** Cheddar cheese, crumbled tortilla chips and chopped tomato.

Pizza Skinny Dips—Try Mozzarella cheese, Parmesan cheese, pizza sauce and chopped salami.

Kaysadillies

Kids really gobble these up and they are so quick and easy to make.

2 tbs. margarine
4 flour tortillas
1 cup shredded Monterey Jack cheese
4 strips bacon, cooked and crumbled (if desired)
guacomole
chopped tomatoes

Heat margarine in skillet. Lay flour tortilla in pan. Quickly spread 1/4 cup cheese and some bacon on half of tortilla. Flip over empty half and cook on medium-high heat until cheese begins to melt. Turn over when bottom is lightly browned. Brown second side. Remove to cool plate, cut into 4 triangles. Repeat with remaining tortillas and filling. Top with guacomole and chopped tomatoes. Makes 4 servings.

Cheese Fondue

Provide the family with skewers and let them dip tonight's dinner.

2 cups shredded sharp Cheddar cheese	1 tsp. dry mustard
1 cup shredded American cheese	1 egg, slightly beaten
3/4 cup milk	1 tbs. margarine

Combine cheese, milk and mustard in top of double boiler. Heat over hot water, stirring constantly until cheese is melted and mixture is blended. Beat in egg and margarine. Cook, stirring, 5 minutes longer. Transfer to fondue pot or warmed bowl. Serve with:

French bread cubes	zucchini strips
toast squares	broccoli pieces
bread sticks	cherry tomatoes
carrot sticks	apple wedges
celery sticks	pear slices
cauliflowerets	

Tuna Half Moons

Another way to present tuna.

1 can (6-1/2 ozs.) tuna, drained
1/2 cup Jack cheese
1/4 cup mayonnaise
1 celery stalk, chopped

1 can (8 ozs.) refrigerator-type biscuits
1 egg
1/2 cup crushed corn flakes

Combine tuna, cheese, mayonnaise and celery. Separate biscuits and put together in twos. Flatten into circles. Spread tuna mixture on top on each circle. Fold to make half moons. Seal by pressing fork into edges. Beat egg and brush onto tops of half moons. Sprinkle with crumbs. Turn and repeat on second side. Bake at 350°F. for 20 minutes. Makes 4 servings.

Note: Look for chunk light tuna, packed in water rather than oil. Some companies are coming out with tuna that is 50% lower in salt.

Tuna Spaghetti

This recipe comes from a mother who lives in Italy. It's a favorite of her three picky-eaters.

1 small garlic clove, chopped
2 tbs. olive oil
3 tbs. chopped parsley
1-1/2 cups canned Italian tomatoes, with their juice, chopped
1 can (10 ozs.) tuna, drained
3 tbs. butter
1 pound spaghetti, cooked

Saute garlic in oil until lightly colored. Add parsley. Stir and cook 30 seconds. Add tomatoes and juice. Simmer uncovered over low heat 25 minutes. Stir occasionally. Break tuna into small pieces. Add to sauce, mixing well. Remove from heat and stir in butter. Serve over cooked spaghetti. Makes 4 servings.

Note: Buy enriched spaghetti made from spinach or other vegetables whenever possible.

Tuna Spaghetti (page 176)
Eskimo Fruit (page 82) ▶

Popeye Burgers

Use any vegetable to enrich burgers. Sneaky—but it works!

1 cup spinach (or green beans, peas, etc.)
1 pound ground beef

Steam vegetable and puree in the blender. Add to ground beef and mix lightly but well. Form into patties and broil. Serve with or without buns.

Peanut Butter Pizza

1/2 cup peanut butter
4 English muffin halves
8 slices bacon, cooked, drained and crumbled

Spread peanut butter on muffin halves. Top with crumbled bacon. Broil until peanut butter is bubbly. Makes 2 to 4 servings.

Turkey Circles

4 turkey franks
4 hamburger buns

1 can (8 ozs.) baked beans

Slash each turkey frank at 1/2-inch intervals, cutting half way through. Broil or barbeque until frank curls into a circle. Heat beans. Place a turkey circle on the bottom half of each bun. Fill centers of circles with 2 tablespoons baked beans. Cover with top bun. Makes 4 sandwiches.

Gobble "Wienies"

2 turkey franks
2 strips Cheddar cheese (1/2 by 3 inches)

2 slices bacon

Cut a lengthwise slit in each turkey frank. Fit strip of cheese into slit. Wrap bacon around each stuffed frank. Fasten with toothpick. Broil or barbeque until bacon is cooked and is brown, turning frequently. Makes 2 servings.

Edible Liver

If liver is "inedible" to your children, this will be a surprise.

1 pound beef liver
1/4 cup flour
1/4 cup soy sauce
1/4 cup water
1 onion, sliced
3 tbs. oil
2 cups rice, cooked

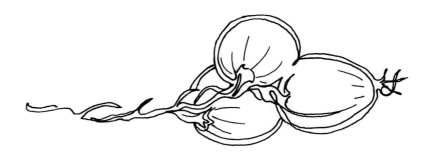

Slice liver into strips. Dust with flour. Mix soy sauce and water. Saute onion in oil. Add liver and brown quickly. Reduce heat. Stir in soy sauce mixture and cook until thickened. Serve over rice. Makes 4 servings.

Cowboy Leather

As long as you don't mention the word L-I-V-E-R, you have a good chance of getting it down their throats. Dip strips in catsup if all else fails.

1 pound liver, cut into 1/2-inch strips
1/2 cup cornmeal, cereal crumbs, bread crumbs, Parmesan cheese
    or combinations
1/4 cup instant nonfat dry milk
1/2 tsp. **each** salt, garlic and onion powder (if desired)
1 tsp. butter **or** margarine

Place liver, cornmeal, dry milk and seasonings in paper bag and shake. Melt butter in non-stick skillet. Fry liver sticks 2 to 3 minutes until browned on both sides.

Pasta Pudding

This is a very popular choice for breakfast, too.

2 tbs. butter
1/4 pound spaghetti, noodles,
  or other pasta, cooked
2 eggs
1 cup milk
1/2 cup yogurt
1/4 cup raisins
1/2 tsp. vanilla
1 tbs. honey (if desired)

Topping:
  3 tbs. butter, melted
  1 cup rolled oats
  1 cup coconut
  1 tbs. honey
  1 tsp. cinnamon

Melt butter in the oven in a 12- by 8-inch pan. Stir remaining ingredients together in mixing bowl. Add 1-1/2 tablespoons melted butter. Pour noodle mixture into buttered pan. Bake at 350°F. for 10 minutes. Mix topping ingredients. Spread over noodles. Reduce temperature to 325°F. Bake 35 minutes longer. Makes 4 servings.

Yummie Yogurts

A healthy ending to any meal, these tasty combinations can also serve as salads or even an afternoon snack.

1 small container lemon yogurt
1 small orange, sectioned
1 tbs. sunflower seeds
1 carrot, shredded

   Mix and serve.

1 small container vanilla yogurt
1/2 cup blueberries, raspberries
   or boysenberries
2 tbs. walnuts

   Mix and serve.

1 small container strawberry yogurt
1/4 cup Rice Krispies
1 banana, sliced

   Mix and serve.

Petite Apple Tarts

Complaints from the family that there's never any dessert?

2 tbs. cornstarch
1 tsp. cinnamon
1/4 tsp. nutmeg
1 cup frozen apple juice concentrate
1 tbs. lemon juice
1 tbs. margarine
6 cups sliced unpeeled apples
6 little pastry **or** graham cracker shells

Blend cornstarch, cinnamon, nutmeg, apple juice and lemon juice together in saucepan. Cook over medium heat until thickened. Add butter. Place apple slices in shells, divided evenly. Pour slightly cooled apple juice mixture over apples. Bake in 350°F. oven for 30 to 40 minutes.

Acknowledgments:

I would like to thank the following people for their assistance in providing me with recipes and up-to-date information on the subject of healthy eating: Helen Torbet, Nutritionist; Joan Kramer, R.N. and Shellie Jerome, Parent-Infant Educators; Colleen Dukes, R.N. and Patti Holmes, Childbirth Educators; Sara Monser, Family Life Instructor; Constance Pike; and Stephen Bail, Child Educator; Linda Lilly, Dental Hygienist; Jackie Walsh, my editor! A special thanks to my many contributing mothers and cooks including: Ann Arns, Lynne Bock-Wilmas, Lucy Galen, Milanna Kerr, Judy Kronmiller, Melanie MacLeod, Deanna Mitchell, Donna Mykrantz, Kathy Ramirez, Barbara Swec, and Mary Warner.

Index

METRIC CONVERSION CHART

Liquid or Dry Measuring Cup (based on an 8 ounce cup)

1/4 cup = 60 ml
1/3 cup = 80 ml
1/2 cup = 125 ml
3/4 cup = 190 ml
1 cup = 250 ml
2 cups = 500 ml

Liquid or Dry Measuring Cup (based on a 10 ounce cup)

1/4 cup = 80 ml
1/3 cup = 100 ml
1/2 cup = 150 ml
3/4 cup = 230 ml
1 cup = 300 ml
2 cups = 600 ml

Liquid or Dry Teaspoon and Tablespoon

1/4 tsp. = 1.5 ml
1/2 tsp. = 3 ml
1 tsp. = 5 ml
3 tsp. = 1 tbs. = 15 ml

Temperatures

°F		°C
200	=	100
250	=	120
275	=	140
300	=	150
325	=	160
350	=	180
375	=	190
400	=	200
425	=	220
450	=	230
475	=	240
500	=	260
550	=	280

Pan Sizes (1 inch = 25 mm)

8-inch pan (round or square) = 200 mm x 200 mm
9-inch pan (round or square) = 225 mm x 225 mm
9 x 5 x 3-inch loaf pan = 225 mm x 125 mm x 75 mm
1/4 inch thickness = 5 mm
1/8 inch thickness = 2.5 mm

Pressure Cooker

100 Kpa = 15 pounds per square inch
70 Kpa = 10 pounds per square inch
35 Kpa = 5 pounds per square inch

Mass

1 ounce = 30 g
4 ounces = 1/4 pound = 125 g
8 ounces = 1/2 pound = 250 g
16 ounces = 1 pound = 500 g
2 pounds = 1 kg

Key   (America uses an 8 ounce cup - Britain uses a 10 ounce cup)

ml = milliliter
l = liter
g = gram
K = Kilo (one thousand)
mm = millimeter
m = milli (a thousandth)
°F = degrees Fahrenheit

°C = degrees Celsius
tsp. = teaspoon
tbs. = tablespoon
Kpa = (pounds pressure per square inch)
This configuration is used for pressure cookers only.

Metric equivalents are rounded to conform to existing metric measuring utensils.